THE

color

GARDEN

(b l u e)

THE color GARDEN

(blue)

single color plantings
for dramatic landscapes

TEXT & PHOTOGRAPHY BY ELVIN McDONALD
INTRODUCTION BY BRIDE M. WHELAN

Collins Publishers San Francisco
A Division of HarperCollins Publishers

A Packaged Goods Incorporated Book

First published 1995 by
Collins Publishers San Francisco
1160 Battery Street
San Francisco, CA 94111-1213

Conceived and produced by
Packaged Goods Incorporated
9 Murray Street, New York, NY 10007
A Quarto Company

Design by Stephen Fay
Endpapers by Michael Levine
Series Editor: Kristen Schilo

Seeds © Copyright 1995 White Swan Ltd., Beaverton, OR. White Swan® and Garden Accents® are registered trademarks of White Swan Ltd.

McDonald, Elvin.
    The color garden (blue) : single color plantings for dramatic landscapes / text & photographs by Elvin McDonald.
        p.   cm.
    Includes Index.
    ISBN 0-00-225085-3
    1. Blue gardens.   I. Title.
SB454.3.C64M37 1995
635.9'68—dc20   94-38702
                                                              CIP

Color separations by Wellmak Printing Press Limited
Printed and bound in Hong Kong by Sing Cheong Printing Co. Ltd.
Photo page 21 by K. SAHIN, Zaden B.V.
Bottom photo page 23 by Environmental Seed Producers

10 9 8 7 6 5 4 3 2 1

blue's for C.Z.
Susan B.
the sky
sweet violets
forget-me-nots
the blue-and-white room
butterfly bush
butterflies
Jerry Sedenko
Ken Neumeyer

Thanks...

to the gardeners who permitted me to photograph their gardens:

Antique Rose Emporium, Brenham, TX; Jean Atwater, Spokane, WA; John Brookes, Denman's Garden, England; Brooklyn Botanic Garden, Brooklyn, NY; The Chelsea Flower Show, London, England; Clause Seeds, Bretigny-sur-Orge, France; The Conservatory Garden, Central Park, New York, NY; Richard Goula, Lafayette, LA; Great Dixter, England; Grigsby Cactus Gardens, Vista, CA; C.Z. Guest, Old Westbury, NY; Hortus Botanicus, Leiden, The Netherlands; Logee's Greenhouses, Danielson, CT; Longwood Gardens, Kennett Square, PA; Los Angeles State and County Arboretum, Arcadia, CA; Lygon Arms, Broadway, The Cotswolds, England; Madderlake, New York, NY; Bickie McDonnell, Memphis, TN; Mercer Arboretum and Botanic Gardens, Humble, TX; University of Minnesota Landscape Arboretum, Chanhassen, MN; University of Minnesota, St. Paul, MN; Montreal Botanical Garden, Montreal, Quebec, Canada; Moody Gardens, Galveston, TX; National Wildflower Research Center, Austin, TX; New York Botanical Garden, Bronx, NY; John F. Noblitt, Fire Island, NY; Oxford Botanical Garden, Oxford, England; George W. Park Seed Co., Inc., Greenwood, SC; Plum Creek Farm, Sharon, CT; Virginia Robinson Garden, Beverly Hills, CA; Sissinghurst Castle Gardens, England; Strybing Arboretum, San Francisco, CA; Wave Hill, Bronx, NY.

Cape forget-me-not (*Anchusa capensis*) in cultivars like 'Blue Angel' and 'Blue Bird' is among the bluest of annuals.

contents

introduction

$\mathcal{T}$he classic cool of blue reminds us of languid summer days, long swims and an endless cape of sky. The tall delphiniums *(page 32)* of summer and the blue-violet asters *(page 16)* of fall capture in part the easy momentum of the blue palette garden, which reaches its zenith in mid-summer with the perennial iris and hortensia.

The harmony in a monochromatic garden is particularly apparent when blue is at its center. It is widely held that a blue field of vision conveys an overall sense of tranquillity. The opposite of the red garden, the blue garden can significantly slow the pulse rate, reduce body temperature, and limit the appetite.

Blue sends an unmistakable message of calm and serenity. Sky and sea surround our world and this blueness gives comfort and assurance. Blue, whatever its tint or shade, is the hue most often associated with authority and security, truth and wisdom. It is the safe haven. So it is with a blue garden: we never want to leave.

The shortest wave length of the visible spectrum, blue is flanked by blue-violet and violet on its warm side and blue-green and green on its cool side. A variety of floral possibilities from hydrangeas to pansies to rhododendrons creates a marvelous mix of cool and warm hues, all parented by blue. A blue garden need not be interpreted as dull or lifeless. On the contrary, sublime mixes of reds and yellows within the spectral range of blue create exciting color combinations in a multitude of blue-violet, violet, and blue-green plantings and arrangements. We need only think of bushes of lilacs and vitex, caryopteris and airy forget-me-nots to realize blue is big-hearted enough to welcome wide variety.

The verdant foliage which surrounds the blue garden acts more like a neighbor or close relative rather than a complement. Varied greens, derived from primary blue and yellow, become the dark hunter greens, the pale mint greens, the deep blue-greens that accent and underscore the richness of the flowers within a garden of blue.

Blue is deliberate and grounds you in its space. It is solid. It is forever. Unlike a yellow garden which is always moving and spontaneous, and a red garden which is vigorous and full of life, the blue garden beckons and holds.

BRIDE M. WHELAN

(I)

b e d s a n d b o r d e r s

*B*LUE IS THE MOST POPULAR COLOR. LIKING IT CAN MEAN THAT you are a person who is secure, sensitive, cautious, social, loyal, capable, and totally conscientious. In the garden, blue is a color as indispensable as green, as encouraging as a fair-weather sky, or as comforting as softly faded blue denim. Blue-flowered plants scattered by design all through a garden can have a mystical, tranquilizing effect.

Flowers called blue may be true or sky blue or any permutation between blue and red, including blue-violet, violet, and red-violet. Among the bluest shrubs are ceanothus *(opposite),* vitex, caryopteris, and certain lilacs *(Syringa).* Blue hardy perennials like the globe thistle echinops *(above)* always refresh the view, alone or in the company of complementary colors such as yellow, orange, or pink.

("Pale purple" defines the
color lilac while lilac plants
(Syringa), ranging from
dwarf shrubs to small trees,
yield flowers that can be
lilac-colored, but also every
nuance from bluish-white to
the deep violet-blue of indigo.
A lilac can also be pink
or even yellow. Four
tree-trained Althaea
'Blue Bird' mark a kitchen
garden walk intersection.
Also called rose of Sharon,
it blooms azure in summer.)

Mountain bluet *(shown above)* is *Centaurea montana,* a widely adapted perennial bachelor's-button with starry, thistly-blue daisy flowers beginning in late spring.

The genus *Campanula* is rich in blues, from dark, violet-blues that can be best appreciated on a bright but overcast day, to forthright blues like Canterbury bells or *C. medium (left).* Others pale to the powdery, smoky blues seen in late summer's chimney bellflower, *C. pyramidalis (opposite, upper).* Balloon flower *(Platycodon)* is a bright blue campanula relative *(opposite, lower)* for summer.

🌿 The chimney bellflower (*Campanula pyramidalis*) grows to shoulder-high and more, terminating its many slender arching branches with clusters of showy blue or white flowers, graceful in the garden and elegant for cutting. It grows quickly, and tends to a short life, but self-sows.

🌿 There are also pink and white balloon flowers *(Platycodon grandiflorus)* but it is the blue ones that can play a solid, if not starring role, in summer beds and borders. Since they grow slowly, getting better and better, set three in a clump and repeat to gain synergy.

Alpine aster (*Aster alpinus*) is for rock gardens and tucking between tidy green or gray neighboring plants. The dark lavender rays of cultivar 'Goliath' give a surprisingly bright effect because of their deep yellow centers.

Asters, beginning with the alpines of spring such as *Aster alpinus* 'Goliath' *(opposite page)*, offer a full range of blues all summer and autumn until a killing frost. There are pure white and bright-yellow asters but it is the blue ones that come at the end of summer, species or hybrids of the New England *(A. novae-angliae)* and New York *(A. novi belgii)* asters, that have a way of cheering the garden picture at a time when many plants are dwindling. These come in dwarf, medium, and tall sizes and are often sold budded and blooming in containers. The blue range is strong, from bright to pale or grayed, on to lavender, violet, and dark red-purple. The tall ones are ideal for bouquets with fall foliage.

Pincushion flower *(left, upper)* is a powdery blue in harmony with similarly pastel yellow or pink flowers, or silver leaves. The effect of pale blue can also be heightened by placing it with complementary darker or brighter blues.

Comfrey, the herb *(left, lower)*, is also a worthy border flower. The roots persist, and new ones rise in unexpected places. There is a long or intermittent flowering most of the season. Not for everyone, but the right *Symphytum caucasicum* or *S.* x *uplandicum* makes a bold foliage statement and a refined display of azure to violet-blue bells.

🌿 *Salvia* x *superba* 'East Friesland' is an intense violet-blue that can be arresting lit by the sun of an early summer morning or evening. Pink and orange poppies and lupines share the bed.

Salvias—the sages—are rich in blues and some have silver-blue to purplish leaves. Two of the bluest, possibly least cultivated, are *Salvia azurea,* with graceful spikes of azure, and *S. patens,* large and gentian blue.

'Indigo Spires,' a super-strength, *S. farinacea* type, is nearly always blooming in warm, moist or dry climates. Elsewhere, treat these sages like other marginally hardy or tender species, as annuals, grown yearly from seeds, or perpetuated via cuttings taken in fall and wintered in a warm place.

The salvias pictured show a sampling of four popular species, one widely adapted to extremes of heat and cold ('East Friesland'), two for relatively warm places or wintering-over in containers (*S. guaranitica* and *S. leucantha*), and one (*S. farinacea*) mostly propagated from seeds of superior cultivars, with colors ranging from silvery white to intense, dark blue-violet.

Salvia leucantha (upper left), Mexican bush sage, blooms violet-purple, late summer to frost. *S. guaranitica (upper right),* variously annual or perennial, can bloom nonstop three seasons out of four. *S.* x *superba* 'East Friesland' *(lower left)* also fits a blue-and-white teaming with *Iris pallida* and *Achillea* 'White Beauty.' *Salvia farinacea (lower right),* mealycup sage, from gray-white to dark blue, consorts well with yellows, pinks, and salmons.

(2)

r o c k   g a r d e n   a n d
g r o u n d   c o v e r

ℬLUE FLOWERS THAT CARPET THE GROUND OR FORM LOW mounds in a rock garden can be as welcome as catching a glimpse of sunny blue sky through dark storm clouds. Ajuga or bugle, shown opposite in spring bloom, spends much of the year as a colorful foliage plant and adapts widely to hot and cold. Here, it shares a bed with tall chartreuse euphorbia, small epimedium, silver-striped lamium, and bluish snow-in-summer (*Cerastium*).

Viscaria 'Blue Angel' (*above*) blooms all summer in sun, with cool nights and warm days. Evolvulus 'Blue Daze,' a dwarf bush morning glory, opens fresh, clear blue flowers daily in all kinds of warm weather.

🌿 'Chatahoochee' phlox is a
hybrid between blue phlox *(P.*
divaricata laphamii) and *P. pilosa,*
shown here on sunny steps in front
of blue rosemary *(Rosmarinus).*
This phlox is showy in spring,
fragrant, and favored for well-
drained pots and rock gardens.

There are blue phlox suited to wild and cultivated gardens, for sun and for part shade. Here are some for rock gardens, ground covers, and containers.

Moss pink (*Phlox subulata*) forms a sun-loving mat that is mostly evergreen except when it is obliterated by the spring flowers. Cultivars come in pale to dark lavender blue, on over into the lilacs and red-violets.

Wild blue phlox (*P. divaricata*) has light blue, subtly fragrant flowers in spring. There are several selections, some bluer, some redder, to rose-pink and white. The phlox shown under the swing is in Memphis, Tennessee.

The choice 'Chatahoochee' (in earthen pot, *opposite page*) is a form of *P. pilosa* with red-eyed, lavender-blue flowers. It thrives in moist part shade but tends to bloom out and die if not clipped back, cleaned out, and encouraged a bit after the spring flowering finishes.

California bluebell (*Phacelia campanularia; right*) blooms all summer in sun and takes dryish soil.

(3)

cottage garden

*T*HE HUMBLE ORIGINS OF THE COTTAGE GARDEN HAVE GIVEN IT blues from the beginning. Useful herbs and medicinal plants—rosemary, mint, borage, chicory, lavender *(above)*—have been lacing, edging, and scenting the most personal of gardening styles for hundreds of years. Felicia, the blue daisy *(opposite)*, propagated by cuttings, and self-sowing forget-me-nots like *Anchusa capensis* are typical of the flowers permitted to share beds with the necessities.

Wherever lives a gardener, there will be a cottage garden, a plot of ground next to the dwelling or assemblage of pots by the door. It grows from all manner of seeds, bulbs, roots, offsets, divisions, and "slips" (cuttings benignly poached). While the overall layout may have a plan, where each new occupant is planted has more to do with intuition, available space, or suitable conditions.

The florist, bigleaf, or hortensia hydrangea *(H. macrophylla) (right, upper)* comes to cottage gardens as a seasonal potted flower, often a Mother's Day gift. Established plants can give two flowerings yearly; they need abundant water and acid fertilizer. Wild violets *(right, lower)* are collectibles that have more impact when brought together, as here in a twig basket. They also make tidy bed edgers. Virginia bluebells *(opposite), Mertensia virginica*, suggest a romantic walk through a partly sunny woodland or wild garden. They bloom through mid-spring.

The ability to be self-reliant is, if not a requisite for cottage garden dwellers, a distinct advantage. Plants that volunteer by self-sowing seeds have a way of coming up in unexpected places where you'd never think to put them or wouldn't be able, such as in crevices between paving stones.

After establishing such a plant initially, its future management has more to do with selective weeding and thinning than deliberate planting. By permitting plants to move about the garden serendipitously, fresh soil is gained and vigorous growth assured year after year. This letting go of strict control on the part of the gardener also permits the garden to evolve so as to be endlessly fascinating.

Blue flowers that self-sow are mostly wild species that can survive without pampering but thrive on well-drained soil enriched with compost. Besides the three blue flowers pictured, consider also these: miniature hollyhock, known in the trade as *Althaea zebrina*, which is violet-red; anchusa, a hairy-leaved and bright-blue forget-me-not, to thigh-height, inclined to sprawling unless staked by brushing; borage, the herb, ditto everything said about anchusa, except the flowers are five-pointed azure stars with a touch of pink; collinsia, or blue lips, for partly shaded slopes; myosotis, the most delicately textured forget-me-nots, in light to dark blues, also white and pink; echium, or viper's bugloss, a borage relative with blue or blue-and-rose flowers; light blue globe gilia (*G. capitata);* blue flax, *Linum perenne; Lupinus texensis,* Texas blue bonnet; *Nemophila menziesii,* baby-blue-eyes; *Nigella damascena,* 'Miss Jekyll'; *Phacelia campanularia,* California bluebell; and violas such as the Johnny-jump-up and the miniature pansy 'Baby Lucia.'

Centaurea cyanus or bachelor's button *(above), Consolida* species or larkspur, *(opposite, upper)* and *Eustoma russellianum,* or Texas bluebell *(opposite, lower),* are examples of blue flowers having the ability to volunteer, or self-sow themselves once they become established. Being carefree, they are cottage garden treasures. All three have sported or been hybridized to bloom white, pink, or maroon and one, eustoma, has become the many-splendored *Lisianthus* of the seed trade.

Blue-flowered vines such as *Thunbergia grandiflora, Plumbago capensis,* numerous varieties of *Wisteria* and *Lathyrus* or sweet pea, also *Petrea volubilis, Clitoria,* and *Dolichos*—bring verticality to all kinds of gardens but never more beneficially than in the cottage element. They, along with the blue vines pictured, can be managed in pots or in the ground, on a tepee, fence, wall, lattice or twig trellis, a pergola, gazebo, porch, or mailbox post.

A typical "tepee" is three or four bamboo stakes 6 feet (183 cm) long secured in a triangle or square 18 inches (46 cm) apart by inserting them straight into the ground 6-12 inches (15 to 30 cm) deep, then pulling them together and tying them at the top. Tepees are also constructed in larger and smaller sizes, often by incorporating twigs from the property. This is an ideal way to train the incredibly blue-flowered butterfly pea vine, *Clitoria ternatea,* and the fragrant purple hyacinth bean, *Dolichos lablab*—both quick to bloom from seeds in hot weather—and for every blue through a cool season from fragrant sweet peas, *Lathyrus odoratus.* (The more you gather for nosegays and little bouquets, the more profusely the pea vines will bloom.)

The blue-flowered vines *opposite, clockwise,* include, *beginning top left:* potato vine, *Solanum seaforthianum,* a warm-climate species that blooms all year; wisteria's lavender-blue flowers are also fragrant; morning glory, *Ipomoea purpurea* 'Heavenly Blue,' on a lattice-shaded greenhouse; Maypop, apricot vine, or passion flower, *Passiflora incarnata,* for warm-weather growing; and early, large-flowered *Clematis* 'Mrs. Cholmondeley,' widely adapted to cold and hot climates.

Overleaf, two indispensable cottage garden blues: larkspur or annual delphinium, *Consolida ambigua, left,* and *on the right-hand page* an azure perennial *Delphinium elatum* of the 'California Giant' strain, with a white and yellow "bee" in each floret center.

Bulb flowers are rich in blue, beginning with spring's first crocus and squills (*Scilla sibirica*), and the English and Spanish bluebells (*Hyacinthoides*) that a month or so later grace wild and tended gardens and make fine companions for bluish to purplish hardy geraniums, white sweet woodruff (*Galium odoratum*), and white to lavender-blue late tulips. Hostas are almost ideal since their decorative leaves unfold precisely on time to hide the maturing bulb foliage.

Between the earliest and latest spring bulb blues are some of the truest basic blues: *Chionodoxa*, Dutch hyacinths, grape hyacinths (*Muscari*), and the 'Atrocaerulea' variety of *Anemone blanda*.

Besides numerous alliums for summer blues, there are the blue ginger (*Dichorisandra thyrsiflora*), lavender-blue peacock ginger (*Kaempferia roscoeana*), blue florist gloxinia (*Sinningia*), blue true gloxinia (*Gloxinia perennis*), and blue cultivars of nut orchid (*Achimenes*).

The big show for blue bulb flowers is from lily-of-the-Nile, the potentially imposing *Agapanthus* that in its largest varieties can stand boldly waist-high with huge spheres of blue flowers rising above like fireworks. There is also a dwarf, *A. africanus* 'Minor,' the Peter Pan lily, that grows only knee-high, but still packs a blue punch.

Bulbs such as English and Spanish bluebells (*Hyacinthoides*, also known as *Scilla* and *Endymion*) have become a part of the charm associated with cottage gardens, perhaps an extension of the pleasure found in such useful bulbous plants as blue-pink chives (*Allium schoenoprasum*) and its host of blue-flowered relatives embraced by the lily family.

The iris family includes some of the cottage gardener's most beloved blue flowers, the precise species favored being somewhat dependent on the local climate. Fortunately, the clan is widely adapted, with blue-flowered species or cultivars of one kind or another suited to just about all kinds of gardens, hot or cold, wet or dry, sunny or partly shaded.

Early in the spring in woodland or wild garden settings there is the crested dwarf *Iris cristata* that grows wild from rhizomes in the northeast United States and varies from blue to lilac. Similarly early, from corms, is the diminutive *I. reticulata* (deep violet to mid- or light blue, lightly scented) and the taller English, Dutch, and Spanish iris, representing different species and hybrids but bearing a distinct resemblance to one another, and rich in some of the floral kingdom's most royal and refined blues.

Irisarians in warmer regions have no finer source of spring blues than the splendid Louisiana iris, while those in colder climates can rejoice in the embarassment of riches to be found among the tall beardeds *(I. germanica)*, illustrated left and opposite, and the Siberians *(I. sibirica)*. Wherever there is adequate water during the main growing season, in any climate, the Japanese iris *(I. ensata)* will, in its moment at the beginning of summer, eclipse everything else in the garden, blue or otherwise.

Tall bearded or German iris, *I. germanica*, come in some of the most breathtaking blues that can be brought into a garden. There are the solid blues like the one next to a picket fence, *above*, and a dazzling array of bicolors featuring blue and white, *examples opposite, far left.*

(4)

the butterfly garden

 UTTERFLIES ARE EQUIPPED TO DINE ON THE NECTAR FOUND IN certain throated blossoms, such as those of verbena *(opposite)* and buddleia *(above)*, the latter so irresistible that it is known as the butterfly bush.

Verbenas of the vervain type such as *V. rigida* grow thigh-high and form tuberous roots that become their means of survival through drought and freezing weather. They flower over a long season, are widely adapted, and make attractive ground covering for a sunny hillside.

Buddleia davidii cultivars span the blue spectrum from the clear pastel blue of 'Lochinch' to the midnight blue-purple of 'Black Knight.' There is, in addition, a full range of colors that includes lilac, lavender, pink, and snowy white. These fast-growing shrubs bloom on new growth, midsummer and continue to frost.

Borage, the herb, *Borago officinalis*, blooms its starry blue and pink (edible) flowers over a long season.

Butterfly plants have taken on new meaning as more and more gardeners have given up the use of poisonous pesticides. Butterfly sitings could include a Giant Swallowtail, North America's largest butterfly, come to dine on woods or Louisiana phlox, or the Gulf Fritillary on blue passion flower *(Passiflora)*.

The Great Spangled Fritillary favors thistles, bee-balm, vetch, and verbena, all of which include blue, bluish, or lavender-blue flowers. Silver and blue Spring Azure is often seen on spring blues ceanothus and viola.

Monarch butterflies bring their brilliant orange wings to accent the beauty of such blue flowers as buddleia, lilac, and mint, and also to the red-violet or magenta Joe-Pye weed *(Eupatorium)*, and gay feather *Liatris*.

Other blues for the butterfly garden include *Hebe*, germander *(Teucrium)*, lavender *(Lavandula)*, chaste tree *(Vitex)*, bluebeard *(Caryopteris)*, creeping phlox *(P. subulata)*, Jacob's ladder *(Polemonium)*, cupid's dart *(Catananche caerulea)*, sea holly *(Eryngium)*, Michaelmas daisies *(Aster)*, ageratum, heliotrope *(Heliotropium)*, lupine *(Lupinus)*, forget-me-not *(Myosotis)*, and petunias.

Chicory *(opposite)* is one of the bluest flowers seen by roadsides in temperate and subtropical parts of the world. It is cultivated in gardens as *Cichorium intybus* and may be harvested as Belgian endive or radicchio before it comes into bloom.

(5)

c o m p l e m e n t a r y   c o l o r
s c h e m e s

*B*LUE, THE GARDEN'S MOST SOOTHING COLOR, THE PEACEMAKER between flowers whose hues might otherwise clash, often achieves its greatest beauty in the presence of a complementary color. The blue and pink Cape primroses *(above)*, hybrids of *Streptocarpus*, are so harmonious it seems apparent that they are from the same set of paints, one comprised of more blue, the other of more red.

The azure of annual bedding *Lobelia erinus* 'Cambridge Blue' *(opposite)*, gives fair sky color under the salmon-pink annual *Phlox drummondii*, a subtle variation on the blue-and-pink theme. This scheme is warm, friendly, and confident.

Blue and red combinations fairly sing when the hues balance, as illustrated by the terra cotta pot of glowing rosy red, lily-flowered tulips and innocent blue forget-me-nots *(near right)*, photographed at Sissinghurst Castle gardens in England at spring's peak.

By the same rule of color balance, the saturated blue-purple petunias *(opposite)* with vivid, slightly orange-red hybrid geraniums *(Pelargonium)*, in wooden planter boxes on a sun-struck deck near the Atlantic Ocean at Fire Island, New York, are entirely harmonious. Their gaudy brilliance also fits a summer retreat.

These seeming extremes of locale and variations on the blue-and-red theme illustrate a primary point about color gardens of this type: Often the hues of spring will be paler while those of summer and autumn go deeper, a natural response to the strength and direction of sun rays. When synergy develops between the principal blues and reds, the result will be more than the sum of its parts.

Glowing rosy red, lily-flowered tulips and *Myosotis* forget-me-nots grace a large terra cotta pot. Clean, bright colors like these look most radiant in the hopeful light of spring.

Saturated blue-purple hybrid
grandiflora petunias look
smashing with similarly vivid red
hybrid geraniums (Pelargonium) lit
by a touch of orange for wooden
boxes at a beach house.

Blue flowers and silver leaves together are a combination many gardeners find irresistible. A spring favorite is blue or red-violet woods phlox, also known as Louisiana phlox, and the silver-white leaves of lamb's-ears *(Stachys byzantina)*. Later, after the phlox is quietly vegetating, the silvery lamb's-ears will look perfect with blue ageratum or silene, 'Lavender Lady' gomphrena, or clear sky-blue multiflora petunias. There is a silver-leaved ajuga sufficiently metallic to help mark a garden walk at dawn or dusk.

Plants that have silver leaves are by nature sun lovers. Their roots also need perfect drainage. Often they are adapted to relatively moist springs and dry summers, making them suited to the way things really are in a vast number of gardens. Add to this the blue flowers that respond vigorously to the same set of conditions, and soon a blue-and-silver theme can develop, by investing as the seasons pass in locally adapted plants that provide silver or blue—or both—as in the grayish-leaved, blue-flowered caryopteris.

Silver foliages can be spun through a garden like so much silver thread, a quiet under theme that stands out a bit after dark or sometimes with surprising luminosity on a gray day. There are several artemisias that can do this, from the petite 'Silver Mound,' to the knee-high, lacy, and sweetly scented 'Powis Castle,' and taller, coarser, 'Silver King.' Russian sage *(Perovskia atriplicifolia)* gives a similar effect until the gray-ghostly plants become covered with countless tiny azure flowers.

The gardens pictured opposite also include a secondary or complementary element of red, the deep redness of barberry *(Berberis)* leaves as a backdrop and 'Lavender Lady' gomphrena.

Blue-and-silver combinations take on new dimensions joined by pink-lavender or the dark red of barberry *(Berberis)*, as shown in the photographs *opposite*, both taken at the Conservatory Garden in Central Park, New York City. The *upper picture* features all hardy perennials, five-starred blue balloon flowers *(Platycodon)*, a silver-blue cloud from Russian sage *(Perovskia)*, blue rose of Sharon *(Althaea)*, and deep-red-leaved barberry as backdrop. The *lower picture* features the scheme in annuals: blue mealycup sage *(Salvia)*, 'Lavender Lady' gomphrena, and silver-leaved, tender perennial *Helichrysum petiolare*.

Blue-and-white is a garden
color theme repeated over and
over in nature, within the
same flower, the blue-and-
white pansies here, or in the
juxtaposition of wildflowers
like the white prickly poppy
(above), Argemone albiflora,
in a field of blue salvia.
Glazed blue-and-white
Oriental garden pots
strategically placed can help
underscore the scheme.

Blue delphinium and orange calendula *(above)*; a marriage made in heaven—blue's spiritual counterpart. Blue is orange's direct opposite on the color wheel and this dynamism makes for a dramatic garden. Evolvulus 'Blue Daze' *(opposite)* and orange glow vine *(Senecio confusus)* team intensely in summer weather.

Blue's direct opposite on the color wheel is orange. Placed next to each other in the garden the attraction of opposites becomes the stuff of which strong garden color themes are born... and then encouraged year after year by planting more or better of the chosen hues. The addition of blue's near-complementary colors, yellow-orange and red-orange, with blue itself expressed in similar shades, can add up to an endlessly vivid, stimulating, and reassuring garden.

Delphiniums and their annual counterparts the larkspurs *(Consolida)* are rather the standards by which blue spire flowers are judged. This does not mean they are the only ones. There are also some exceptional blue veronicas, monkshood *(Aconitum)*, penstemon, bellflower campanulas, and platycodon.

Calendulas bloom best in cool but frost-free weather. When summer turns hot, marigolds of the *Tagetes* type come in every yellow, gold, and orange imaginable for blue's company.

Lemon-yellow lilies *(Lilium)* and blue-flowered hostas with chartreuse foliage harmonize at their zenith in midsummer. The simple white arbor adds architectural interest.

Summer is by color yellow and blue—yellow for abundant sun and blue for fair skies. So it seems not surprising that this combination makes for beautiful gardens beginning with springtime landscapes filled with blues and yellows. It is at high summer, however, and on toward fall that the combination really comes into its own, through hybrid lilies, Maxmilian sunflowers, and hostas, the latter blue- or golden chartreuse-leaved and often having lavender-blue flowers.

🐦 Daylilies *(Hemerocallis)* are possibly the single richest source for yellow flowers to complement every blue imaginable, here the violet-blue of statice *(Limonium).*

The many facets of blue, from reddish magenta through sky blue and azure, darkening to deep purple, have a ready supply of complementary colors among the modern daylilies *(Hemerocallis).* Originally yellow or orange, today's hybrids come in every imaginable color and rank among the garden designer's largest choice of colors from a single genus. Set in front of blues such as statice *(Limonium),* lavender *(Lavandula),* or rosemary *(Rosmarinus),* they are certain to please.

(6)

leaves and fruit

B LUE IS NOT FOR SKIES, FLOWERS, LAKES, AND BIRDS ALONE. There are numerous blue leaves and fruit that once appreciated can express uncommon beauty. There are, for example, in the genus *Senecio* numerous succulent species resembling the one pictured *(opposite)*, whose cylindrical and evenly ascending leaves are ghostly blue-green on stems the same color.

Echeveria (above) is a related grouping of succulent plants that are cherished for their beautifully tinted leaves, often appearing as though they are reflecting a desert sky at dawn or sunset.

Blue-fruited ornamentals include porcelain-berry *(Ampelopsis)*, leatherleaf mahonia *(M. bealei)*, and the edible blueberry *(Vaccinium)*. Widely adapted native beautyberry *(Callicarpa)* is bright purple.

Silvery blue-green foliage like that of the dusty miller *(Senecio maritima* 'Silver Dust')* used in the Victorian pattern display shown *(right)* can weave a silver thread through the garden, the effect of which can be gotten from few other plants. Here it joins white candytuft *Iberis,* green dwarf boxwood, pots of white hybrid geranium *(Pelargonium)* and urns spilling over with delicate, white Marguerite daisies *(Chrysanthemum frutescens).*

There are also numerous cultivars of dusty miller, some finely cut or laced, others oakleaf-shaped or plain but no less silvery, an appearance emphasized by sun and being grown hard-stressed a bit between waterings. Several botanical names are applied to plants that look and act like dusty miller: *Cineraria, Senecio, Tanacetum, Pyrethrum,* and *Chrysanthemum.*

While dusty miller is almost always treated as an annual or short-lived perennial, there are also several compact, even shearable silver perennials or subshrubs: *Artemisia (A. absinthium,*

'Powis Castle,' 'Silver Mound') and *Santolina* combine handsomely with blue salvia, verbena, and petunias.

Dittany of Crete, *Origanum dictamnus,* is the true healing herb of legend. It thrives warm and on the dry side in summer, with the best conformation of stacked, blue-silver leaves and hoplike purplish-pink flowers in full sun. The related *O. rotundifolium* 'Kent Beauty' is similar but even showier.

Lamiastrum, Lamium, and *Galeobdolon* are all names used for a grouping of square-stemmed mint relatives that have metallic silver foliage variegation most of the year.

The newest family development in coral bells, *Heuchera,* is silver foliage, notably 'Pewter Veil,' with leaves as extraordinary as any silver-splashed and veined rex begonia.

One of the bluest plants that can be brought into a garden is the vegetable kale, especially the Italian heirloom *Brassica* 'Lacinato,' with deeply crinkled bold foliage that becomes living sculpture in winter.

Origanum dictamnus, the herb known as Dittany of Crete *(above),* has downy, blue-silver leaves and purplish-pink flowers. *Lamiastrum* 'Silver Sweet' *(below)* and the related *Lamium* are noteworthy for metallic silver leaves on low plants.

(7)

e x o t i c   b l u e s

*D*AY-BLOOMING TROPICAL WATER LILIES (*NYMPHAEA*) ARE exceptional for blue, from the intense blue-purple of 'Blue Triumph' to the periwinkle of 'Charles Thomas' or the bright blue of the profuse and fragrant 'Blue Beauty.' Floating water plants such as the water hyacinth (*above*) have blue flowers best appreciated up close in a garden pond. For a submersed pot or bog there is the blue-flowered pickerel rush (*Pontederia cordata*).

Blue-flowered cultivars of German primrose (*Primula obconica; opposite*) bloom in cool but not freezing weather. Among tropicals, the *Vanda* orchids can be amazingly blue. Parrot-blue fruit ripens in the boat-shaped bracts of the *Heliconia* and the bird-of-paradise *Strelitzia reginae* combines peacock blue with brilliant orange.

Vanda coerulea orchids set the standard for flower blues among tropicals the way the German iris does for temperate plants. Both display a range of blues taken from fair to stormy skies and often include a second color. The clear and brighter blue vandas look well in the company of white or yellow flowers, while the stormier, darker, or even muddied shades can come alive with orange, copper, or cream—from surrounding plants or furnishings.

Otacanthus coeruleus, the Brazilian snapdragon, produces clusters of lightly scented blue flowers with white signal patches on the lip. The plants grow and bloom in warm weather to knee-high or so and make a show in medium-size pots. They must be wintered in a warm spot—no chilling allowed—but in reasonably balmy conditions the blue flowers appear for months on end.

🌿 The fruits of *Heliconia* are usually blue or violet, preceded by extraordinary flowers borne from waxy, long-lasting bracts that can be as brightly colored as any of nature's creatures. The plants are tropical and banana-like, for growing in constantly warm and humid conditions.

🌹 *Brunfelsia australis* is the yesterday-today-and-tomorrow plant that blooms from spring to fall. The sweetly scented flowers open deep blue-violet, then pale to near white. It needs sun, water, and nutrients.

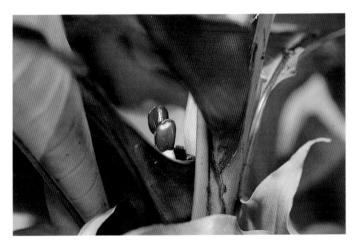

🌹 Blue poppy (*Meconopsis*), photographed with German iris at the Chelsea Flower Show, is among the bluest found in nature, mostly in the Himalayas, and in mild-climate gardens.

Fan flower, *Scaevola aemula*, a recent arrival in cultivation, has white-eyed blue flowers reminiscent of lobelia. Unlike bedding lobelia, *L. erinus*, however, it goes on blooming in hot, humid weather, and may even welcome winter if there has not been a sharp freeze. Scaevola is ideal for planting to spill from baskets, boxes, and large pots.

Eranthemum pulchellum has terminal spikes of brilliant blue flowers in winter to spring and easily colonizes in warm-climate gardens. Elsewhere it can be potted for a sunny window, greenhouse, or conservatory.

Coleus (or *Plectranthus*) *thyrsoideus* is another winter-to-spring blue, with spikes of delphinium-blue flowers above leaves that smell pungent when lightly brushed or pinched.

Clerodendrum ugandense is a rapid-growing shrub with panicles of French-blue and marine-blue flowers in summer; in winter keep potted in a warm place.

sources

Jacques Amand
P.O. Box 59001
Potomac, MD 20859
free catalog; all kinds of bulbs

Amaryllis, Inc.
P.O. Box 318
Baton Rouge, LA 70821
free list; hybrid Hippeastrum

Antique Rose Emporium
Rt. 5, Box 143
Brenham, TX 77833
*catalog $5; old roses; also
perennials, ornamental grasses*

B & D Lilies
330 "P" Street
Port Townsend, WA 98368
catalog $3; garden lilies

Kurt Bluemel
2740 Greene Lane
Baldwin, MD 21013
*catalog $2; ornamental grasses;
perennials*

Bluestone Perennials
7237 Middle Ridge
Madison, OH 44057
free catalog; perennials

Borboleta Gardens
15980 Canby Avenue, Rt. 5
Faribault, MN 55021
*catalog $3; bulbs, tubers, corms,
rhizomes*

Brand Peony Farms
P.O. Box 842
St. Cloud, MN 56302
free catalog; peonies

Breck's
6523 N. Galena Road
Peoria, IL 61632
free catalog; all kinds of bulbs

Briarwood Gardens
14 Gully Lane, R.F.D. 1
East Sandwich, MA 02537
list $1; azaleas, rhododendrons

W. Atlee Burpee Co.
300 Park Avenue
Warminster, PA 18974
*free catalog; seeds, plants, bulbs,
supplies; wide selection*

Busse Gardens
5873 Oliver Avenue S.W.
Cokato, MN 55321
catalog $2; perennials

Canyon Creek Nursery
3527 Dry Creek Road
Oroville, CA 95965
catalog $2; silver-leaved plants

Carroll Gardens
Box 310
Westminster, MD 21158
*catalog $2; perennials, woodies,
herbs*

Coastal Gardens
4611 Socastee Boulevard
Myrtle Beach, SC 29575
catalog $3; perennials

The Cummins Garden
22 Robertsville Road
Marlboro, NJ 07746
*catalog $2; azaleas,
rhododendrons, woodies*

Daylily World
P.O. Box 1612
Sanford, FL 32772
*catalog $5; all kinds of
hemerocallis*

deJager Bulb Co.
Box 2010
South Hamilton, MA 01982
free list; all kinds of bulbs

Tom Dodd's Rare Plants
9131 Holly Street
Semmes, AL 36575
*list $1; trees, shrubs, extremely
select*

Far North Gardens
16785 Harrison Road
Livonia, MI 48154
*catalog $2; primulas, other
perennials*

Howard B. French
Box 565
Pittsfield, VT 05762
free catalog; bulbs

Gardens of the Blue Ridge
Box 10
Pineola, NC 28662
catalog $3; wildflowers and ferns

D.S. George Nurseries
2515 Penfield Road
Fairport, NY 14450
free catalog; clematis

**Glasshouse Works
Greenhouses**
Church Street, Box 97
Stewart, OH 45778
catalog $2; exotics for containers

Greenlee Ornamental Grasses
301 E. Franklin Avenue
Pomona, CA 91766
catalog $5; native and ornamental grasses

Greer Gardens
1280 Goodpasture Is. Rd.
Eugene, OR 97401
catalog $3; uncommon woodies, especially rhododendrons

Grigsby Cactus Gardens
2354 Bella Vista Drive
Vista, CA 92084
catalog $2; cacti and other succulents

Growers Service Co.
10118 Crouse Road
Hartland, MI 48353
list $1; all kinds of bulbs

Heirloom Old Garden Roses
24062 N.E. Riverside Drive
St. Paul, OR 97137
catalog $5; old garden, English, and winter-hardy roses

J.L. Hudson, Seedsman
P.O. Box 1058
Redwood City, CA 94064
catalog $1; nonhybrid flowers, vegetables

Jackson and Perkins
1 Rose Lane
Medford, OR 97501
free catalog; roses, perennials

Kartuz Greenhouses
1408 Sunset Drive
Vista, CA 92083
catalog $2; exotics for containers

Klehm Nursery
Rt. 5, Box 197
Penny Road
South Barrington, IL 60010
catalog $5; peonies, hemerocallis, hostas, perennials

M. & J. Kristick
155 Mockingbird Road
Wellsville, PA 17365
free catalog; conifers

Lamb Nurseries
Rt. 1, Box 460B
Long Beach, WA 98631
catalog $1; perennials

Lauray of Salisbury
432 Undermountain Road, Rt. 41
Salisbury, CT 06068
catalog $2; exotics for containers

Lilypons Water Gardens
6800 Lilypons Road
P.O. Box 10
Buckeystown, MD 21717
catalog $5; aquatics

Limerock Ornamental Grasses
R.D. 1, Box 111
Port Matilda, PA 16870
list $3

Logee's Greenhouses
141 North Street
Danielson, CT 06239
catalog $3; exotics for containers

Louisiana Nursery
Rt. 7, Box 43
Opelousas, LA 70570
catalogs $3-$6; uncommon woodies, perennials

Lowe's Own Root Roses
6 Sheffield Road
Nashua, NH 03062
list $5; old roses

McClure & Zimmerman
Box 368
Friesland, WI 53935
free catalog; all kinds of bulbs

Merry Gardens
Upper Mechanic Street, Box 595
Camden, ME 04843
catalog $2; herbs, Pelargoniums, cultivars of Hedera helix

Milaeger's Gardens
4838 Douglas Avenue
Racine, WI 53402
catalog $1; perennials

Moore Miniature Roses
2519 E. Noble Avenue
Visalia, CA 93292
catalog $1; all kinds of miniature roses

Niche Gardens
1111 Dawson Road
Chapel Hill, NC 27516
catalog $3; perennials

Nor'East Miniature Roses
Box 307
Rowley, MA 01969
free catalog

Oakes Daylilies
8204 Monday Road
Corryton, TN 37721
free catalog; all kinds of hemerocallis

Geo. W. Park Seed Co.
Box 31
Greenwood, SC 29747
free catalog; all kinds of seeds, plants, and bulbs

Roses of Yesterday and Today
802 Brown's Valley Road
Watsonville, CA 95076
catalog $3 third class, $5 first; old roses

Seymour's Selected Seeds
P.O. Box 1346
Sussex, VA 23884
free catalog; English cottage garden seeds

Shady Hill Gardens
821 Walnut Street
Batavia, IL 60510
catalog $2; 800 different Pelargonium

Shady Oaks Nursery
112 10th Ave. S.E.
Waseca, MN 56093
catalog $2.50; hostas, ferns, wildflowers, shrubs

Siskiyou Rare Plant Nursery
2825 Cummings Road
Medford, OR 97501
catalog $2; alpines

Anthony J. Skittone
1415 Eucalyptus
San Francisco, CA 94132
catalog $2; unusual bulbs, especially from South Africa

Sonoma Horticultural Nursery
3970 Azalea Avenue
Sebastopol, CA 95472
catalog $2; azaleas, rhododendrons

Spring Hill Nurseries
110 W. Elm Street
Tipp City, OH 45371
free catalog; perennials, woodies, roses

Steffen Nurseries
Box 184
Fairport, NY 14450
catalog $2; clematis

Sunnybrook Farms Homestead
9448 Mayfield Road
Chesterland, OH 44026
catalog $2; perennials, herbs

Surry Gardens
P.O. Box 145
Surry, ME 04684
free list; perennials, vines, grasses, wild garden

Thompson & Morgan
Box 1308
Jackson, NJ 08527
free catalog; all kinds of seeds

Transplant Nursery
1586 Parkertown Road
Lavonia, GA 30553
catalog $1; azaleas, rhododendrons

Van Engelen, Inc.
Stillbrook Farm
313 Maple Street
Litchfield, CT 06759
free catalog; all kinds of bulbs

Andre Viette Farm & Nursery
Rt. 1, Box 16
Fishersville, VA 22939
catalog $3; perennials, ornamental grasses

Washington Evergreen Nursery
Box 388
Leicester, NC 28748
catalog $2; conifers

Wayside Gardens
One Garden Lane
Hodges, SC 29695
free catalog; all kinds of bulbs, woodies, perennials, vines

We-Du Nursery
Rt. 5, Box 724
Marion, NC 28752
catalog $2; uncommon woodies, perennials

White Flower Farm
Box 50
Litchfield, CT 06759
catalog $5; woodies, perennials, bulbs

Gilbert H. Wild and Son, Inc.
Sarcoxie, MO 64862
catalog $3; perennials, peonies, iris, hemerocallis

Yucca Do
P.O. Box 655
Waller, TX 77484
catalog $2; woodies, perennials

index